The Wisdom of
Wallace D. Wattles II

Including:

The Purpose Driven Life

The Law of Attraction

&

The Law of Opulence

The Purpose Driven Life

By Wallace D. Wattles

CONTENTS

Discover the source of power as W. D. Wattles guides you, step-by-step, on the method to achieve 'Cosmic consciousness' in order to bring about the mental and physical conditions you desire. Learn how to successfully use prayer, will, and faith to demonstrate health, wealth, peace and wisdom in your life.

Wealth for All

Our Father has provided the raw material for all the things essential to life, and He has provided a thousand fold more than we can use. The race, taken as a whole, is rich; immensely rich; it is only individuals within the race who are poor. Look at the birds; they have not a fraction of our intelligence; they do not know enough to sow, or reap, or gather provision for the future; and yet they have no famine. The only fear and anxiety are to be found among men.

The satisfaction of human needs is a problem of machinery and organization, and the machinery is pretty well perfected; it is now, then, a matter of organization.

The birds know no anxiety; they live in the Father's kingdom. They all, alike, have access to the Supply. There is no bug trust, and no shrewd bird has, as yet, cornered the worm market. When, instead of going freely to the Great Supply, the birds begin to compete for the limited portions of it, there will begin to be an anxiety among them. There can be no Father's kingdom unless all can have equal access to the Great Supply.

Equality and Democracy

If the supply is super-abundant, and all go freely to it, how can anybody have lack? The trouble is that we have our eyes fixed, not on the Abundance, but on the 'pot of gold'. It is as if there were a mountain of gold, to which we might go for wealth, but on our way thither we find a few scattering nuggets which have been washed down by the rains, and we stop to fight for the possession of these fragments, and so lose the whole.

"Love Thy Neighbor"

It is in this light that we must consider God's command to love one's neighbor as one's self. What does it mean, this loving one's neighbor as himself? Suppose my wife and I sit down to lunch; and there is nothing on the table but a crust of bread and a piece of pie. And suppose that I hastily grasp the pie, and say; "My dear, I certainly love you devotedly; I do wish you had some pie, also," and I swallow it, and leave her the crust; have I loved her as myself?

If I love her as myself, I will desire pie for her as intensely as for myself, and I will try as hard to get it for her as for myself.

If I love you as myself, what I try to get for myself I will try to get for you, and what I try to get for my children I will try to get for your children, and I will no more rest under an injustice done to you or yours than if it had been done to me or mine.

And when we all desire for everybody all that we desire for ourselves, what is there for us to do but to stop competing for a part and turn to the abundance of the Great Whole, which is the kingdom of God.

Why Communism Fails

We may here consider for a moment why the communistic experiment failed, and we shall find the reason easy to get at. Communism has always failed, and always will fail, because it interferes with the Great Purpose, which is the complete development of the individual soul. It extinguishes the individual in the mass, and takes all initiative from him. Seeking to prevent him from gaining power over other men, it robs him of power over himself. It destroys individuality for man can develop only by the free proprietary use of everything he is individually capable of using. Capitalism robs the majority of men of the opportunity to make proprietary use of the things necessary for their individual development; Communism would rob all men of this opportunity. In this, both are the opposite of Christian socialism.

Christian Socialism

Socialism would tremendously extend private property. Its cardinal doctrine is that the individual should own, absolutely and without question, everything which he needs or can use individually; and that the right to hold private property should be limited only when we come to those things which a man cannot operate without exploiting other men.

Man, under socialism, may acquire and hold all that he can use for his own development; but he may not own that which makes him master of another man.

As we approach socialism, the millions of families who are now propertyless will acquire and own beautiful homes, with the gardens and the land upon which to raise their food; they will own horses and carriages, automobiles and pleasure yachts; their houses will contain libraries, musical instruments, paintings and statuary, all that a man may need for the soul-growth of himself and his, he shall own and use as he will.

But highways, railroads, natural resources, and the great machines will be owned and operated by organized society, so that all who wish may purchase the product upon equal terms.

Socialism, when properly understood, offers us the most complete individualism, while communism would submerge the individual in the mass.

The Source of Power: Cosmic Consciousness

God is Universal Spirit, working in all, *through all,* and FOR ALL. This spirit makes the sun shine, causes the rain to fall, and is the POWER behind nature; the one and only LIFE; the one and only INTELLIGENCE. Every man is Godlike because it is Spirit which lives in man.

To be conscious of Spirit is to draw close to God. To have my own consciousness so unified with the consciousness of Spirit is cosmic consciousness, and is the source of all power.

Man's Relationship to God

There is one Source who is all the power there is, all the life there is, and all the intelligence there is; and this Spirit has children, who are of the same substances as Himself, and who have power to think independently, and to separate themselves in consciousness from Him.

And the power to think independently implies the possibility of thinking erroneously; if man separates himself in consciousness from God, he is sure to fall into error, for he can see only an infinitesimal portion of the truth.

Man's life, man's power, and man's wisdom decrease in exact proportion to the extent of his separation in consciousness from God.

The method of attaining cosmic consciousness we will consider in the next chapter.

Attaining Cosmic Consciousness

Cosmic consciousness or conscious unity with Eternal Spirit can only be attained by a continuous and sustained effort on the part of man. The extension of consciousness always requires a mental effort; and this mental effort, when it is a seeking for unity with Spirit, constitutes prayer.

Prayer is an effort of the human mind to become acquainted with God. It is not an effort to establish a relationship which does not exist, but to fully comprehend and recognize a relationship which already exists.

Prayer can have but one object, and that is unity with Spirit; for all other things are included in that.

We do not really seek, through prayer, to get health, peace, power or wealth; *we seek to get unity with God;* and when we get unity with God, health, peace, power and wealth are ours without asking. Whoever has full spiritual consciousness has health, peace, power and wealth.

Oneness Through Prayer and Will

We appear to think, live, move and have our being entirely in ourselves and of ourselves; our physical senses deny the existence of a God. God is not found by extending the outward or objective consciousness.

To attain cosmic consciousness, the effort of prayer must be, first to arouse to activity the spirit in man; and second, to unite that spirit in conscious union with God.

The spirit of man - the ego - the man himself, is aroused whenever the will acts.

Only the man himself can will; the first requirement for attaining cosmic consciousness is that one must will to do the will of God.

To will to do the will of the Father, to keep his sayings, to do his works; this was the first step toward unity. And the next was the prayer of faith.

The prayer of faith cannot be offered twice for the same thing. As soon as you have asked, if you have real faith, your prayer changes to an affirmation of possession. Having willed to do the will of God, and having asked God to receive you into Himself, nothing is left you but to declare, "I and my Father are one." The prayer of faith, when uttered, becomes an affirmation of possession. You cannot continue to pray for a thing when you believe that you receive it; you can only return thanks and assert that it is yours.

The Process of Receiving

First, will to do the will of God, and then (2) pray that you may be one with Him; and then (3) affirm, "I and my father are one."

And when you have definitely established in your consciousness the fact of your unity with Spirit, then draw your deductions of health, peace, power and wealth from this fact, and affirm them; otherwise you may not demonstrate them, for while they are all included in the fact of your unity with God, the mere assertion of that may not bring all the corollaries to your consciousness.

So, the general affirmation of unity with God is not sufficiently definite to bring us health, peace, power and wealth; we do not clearly understand that these are included, and it is better to affirm them. But we must be definite and specific in our understanding of the fact of our unity with God.

"There is one Intelligence, and I am one with that Intelligence." Better, but somewhat clumsy.

"There is one MIND, and I am that MIND." That is a most clear-cut and concise statement of the fact; it would be hard to put it more tersely.

 "There is ONE MIND." When you say that, think of the one Intelligence, permeating all things, vitalizing all things, giving coherence and purpose to all things. Get your thought fixed on this MIND, so that it seems to you that you can see and feel it! Then say: "I AM that MIND."

It is that MIND which is speaking, when I speak; which is acting when I act.

I-AM-that-MIND.

It takes affirming and reaffirming to get this fact fixed in consciousness, but all the time you put into the work is most profitably spent. You can well afford to go into the desert to fast and meditate for forty days; you can well afford to spend whole nights in prayer, if by doing so you can arrive at a full consciousness of your unity with God. For then you will have entered the kingdom.

"There is one MIND, and I am that MIND." Say it continuously, and always when you say it, try to comprehend all that it means. You; you who speak, are eternal mind, eternal power, eternal life.

All things are yours, and all things are possible unto you, when once you have banished the false idea of separateness from your consciousness. Your word will be with power, and you will speak as one having authority; you will demonstrate health, power, wealth and wisdom.

And you can bring this about; only faith and continuing in affirmation while you will to do the will of God are required.

Demonstration and Attainment

After you have affirmed and reaffirmed your unity with the One Mind until that unity has become a fact present to your consciousness, the next step is to become Life-conscious.

Understand that the Mind is a living mind; that it is life, itself.

If you are Mind, you are also Life. There is only one Life, which is in all, and through all; and you are that Life.

So, follow your first affirmation with this; "That MIND is eternal, and it is LIFE; I am that MIND, and I am ETERNAL LIFE."

Repeat this until you have thoroughly stamped it upon your mentality, both conscious and subconscious; until you habitually think of yourself as life, and as eternal life. Now, you habitually think of yourself as a dying being, or as one moving on toward age and decay; this is an error, born of holding separate consciousness. Meet every suggestion of age, decay or death with the positive assertion: "I am ETERNAL LIFE."

Health Consciousness

After Life-consciousness is attained, the step to Health-consciousness is easy. The One Mind is the living stuff from which you are made; and it is pure life. Life must be Health; it is inconceivable that an inflow of pure life should carry with it anything but health. A fountain cannot send forth sweet and bitter at the same time. A good tree cannot bring forth corrupt fruit. Light hath no fellowship with darkness.

The One Mind cannot know disease; can have no consciousness of disease.

The consciousness of disease is an error, the result of judging by appearances; and we judge by appearances only so long as we retain the separate consciousness. One cannot be Life-conscious and conscious of disease at the same time; when we become fully life-conscious we lose the disease-consciousness.

So, the next affirmation is; "That Mind knows no disease; I am that Mind and I am HEALTH." Affirm it with faith; it will cure every sickness, if the affirmation is made in the consciousness that you and your Father are one.

Power Consciousness

Next comes power-consciousness; and the affirmation for this is: "That Mind is the source of all POWER, and cannot know doubt nor fear; I am that Mind, and I am PEACE and POWER."

It needs no argument to show that the source of all power cannot be afraid of anything; what could there be for it to be afraid of? Nor can the source of all power have doubts as to its being able to do any conceivable thing, or to cope with any possible combination of circumstances; what is there that all the power there is cannot do?

It is only when you conceive of yourself as separate from this power that you begin to have doubts as to your ability to do things; it is only as you hold this separate consciousness that you can be afraid.

To have power-consciousness gives poise; poise is the peaceful consciousness of power and is the result of affirming unity with power until it becomes a present fact in consciousness.

You cannot keep your heart from being afraid if you retain consciousness of yourself as something apart from Power. So, understand and affirm that you are one with Power.

Wisdom Consciousness

Wisdom-consciousness is next. Power without wisdom may be a dreadful and destructive thing, like the strength of the runaway horse; and power can be constructive only when wisely applied. So we must affirm the fact of our wisdom. The One Mind, being the source of all things, must know all things from the beginning; must know all truth. The mind which knows all truth cannot be mistaken; mistakes are caused by a partial knowledge of the truth. Such a mind cannot know error. Knowing ALL truth, it can only act along the lines of perfect truth; it can only entertain in consciousness the idea of perfect truth.

It cannot know good from evil; it can know only the good. To recognize anything as evil, a mind must have only a partial knowledge, and a limited consciousness. What seems to be evil is always the result of partial knowledge. Where knowledge is perfect, there is no evil; and no one can be conscious of that which does riot exist.

When we become conscious of ALL truth, we lose the consciousness of evil.

With complete consciousness judgment becomes impossible, for there is nothing to judge. You do not have to exercise judgment when you know the right way; you do not sit in judgment on others where there is no evil.

Where evil and error are non-existent, there can be no judgment. To rise above the error of belief in evil, use this affirmation; "That Mind knows only TRUTH, and knows ALL truth; I am that Mind, and I am KNOWLEDGE and WISDOM."

Wealth Consciousness

Having attained consciousness of eternal life, of health, power, and wisdom, what else do you need? Wealth-consciousness – the assurance of affluence, and abundance.

The one Mind is the original substance, from which all things proceed forth. There is only one element; all things are formed of one stuff. Science is now precipitating sugar, coloring matter, and other substances from the atmosphere. The elements which compose all visible nature are in the atmosphere, waiting to be organized into form; and the atmosphere itself is only a condensed and palpable form of the one original substance - Spirit - God.

All things are made from, and made of, one living intelligent substance; One Mind, and you are that Mind. Therefore, you are the substance from which all things are made, and you are also the Power which makes and forms; you are wealth and abundance, for you are all there is.

So, affirm; "All things, created and uncreated, are in that Mind; I am that Mind, and I am WEALTH and PLENTY."

I Am the Way, Truth, Life

Lastly, say; "I am the WAY, and the TRUTH, and the LIFE; the LIGHT in me shines out to bless the world."

This will give you love-consciousness: the will to bless, and the will to love. Eternal life; health; power and peace; wisdom; wealth; and love; when you are conscious of all these, you have attained cosmic consciousness.

Statement of Being

There is one Mind, and I AM that Mind.

That Mind is eternal, and it is Life.

I am that Mind, and I am ETERNAL LIFE. That Mind knows no disease; I am that Mind, and I am HEALTH. That Mind is the source of all Power, and cannot know doubt nor fear; I am that Mind, and I am POWER and PEACE.

That Mind knows only Truth and knows ALL truth; I am that Mind, and I am KNOWLEDGE and WISDOM. All things created and uncreated, are in that Mind; I am that Mind, and I am WEALTH and PLENTY.

I am the WAY, and the TRUTH, and the LIFE; the LIGHT in me shines out to bless the world.

Our Father, Our King

In a certain city, one day, a boy leaped into the air to catch a ball; and to his own astonishment, as well as to that of the bystanders, he did not come down, but kept right on going up, and up, until he passed out of sight into the clouds. On that same day, and in the same city, a child leaped off a table, and floated to the floor like a feather; but on the next day, trying the same experiment, it went crashing through the floor and was dashed to pieces on the hard floor of the cellar. The law of gravitation varied in that city; one day a man might weigh a ton, and the next day only a few ounces; and this was true of all other natural laws. One day, water would put out fire; the next day the water itself took fire, and burned like gasoline. The laws of chemical action and affinity were not constant; you never could make the same thing twice from the same materials. That was a strange town, wasn't it? You wouldn't want to live there!

Now, of course we know that all this is not true. We know that the laws of matter, motion, energy and life are fixed and changeless; that they are just the same all over the earth, and on all the planets and stars; that they are just the same throughout the universe. Did it ever occur to you that that is why we call it a uni-verse. *Uni* means one; it is a universe, a one-i-verse, and not a multi-verse, or many-verse. It is not the battleground of many laws and forces, but the harmonious product of one force and one law. Theologians and physicians have never quite gotten down to this fact yet; it will be a great day for the world when they do. Preachers still insist that it is a duo-verse; that there is a devil who is nearly or quite as strong as God; and doctors believe in disease as an entity; a real, evil something, which has power in itself.

There is no devil, or contending force in nature. This is God's world. The devil cannot make the sun rise or set. He cannot stop the grass from growing or starve the birds; he has not as much power as a scarecrow; he cannot keep the crows out of the corn.

Law is One, and force is One throughout the universe; and now I want to ask you to fix your minds for a moment on this one Law and one Force, and consider another thing in connection with it. I want you to think, first, of our own solar system; of this particular group of planets, circling around our sun. You know that they act upon each other; they attract each other, and we have evidence that this action is very powerful. Consider the attraction of the moon, for instance; of its enormous force, as shown by the movements of the tides. All the other planets act upon us in just that same way, with the varying degrees of power. Suppose three or four of them should happen to get together in the same general direction, and all exert their "pull" on us at once; do you know what would happen? Why, the earth would be pulled out of its orbit, and the others out of *their* orbits; and they would all go crashing together in one tremendous ruin. Tell me why this hasn't happened; tell me why, when there is an attraction brought to bear upon us on one side, there is always a counter attraction of exactly equal force brought to bear upon us on the other side; who sees to it that this is done, and that the equilibrium is forever maintained?

Bear in mind, also, that our sun itself is in motion; that our planetary system, with all the other suns and stars and systems is sweeping on in one tremendous cycle of magnitude incomprehensible; that the whole universe is circling around a center; and remember that each body exerts an actual attractive force upon all the others. Some bodies larger, and some smaller; some moving in large circles, and others in smaller circles; you can see that the combination of "pulls" they exert upon each other must be endlessly changing; and yet the equilibrium must be exactly maintained, for upon the least overbalancing, world will crash into world, sun into sun, and star into star, until all are in chaos. Who regulates all this? Who brings the right world into the right place, at the right time? Is it done by Law? You might as well talk of a law by the operation of which, when one reached a certain corner, the streetcar one wanted should be always just coming!

The study of the universe forces us to one admission; and that is that the universal Force possesses the attribute of Directivity; and by directivity I mean the power to bring the right body to the right place at the right time. Now, can you conceive of such a thing as directivity without intelligence? You cannot do it; you cannot conceive of a blind, unintelligent force as making these endless combinations and re-combinations of Planets and systems; there is a Mind of the universe, and that is God.

If, now, we concede to this intelligence the power to control the movements of the heavenly bodies, we must concede to it all other power; for all the so-called forces are but different phases of manifestation of the One force. The directivity we see in the atoms in the crucible is universal directivity; the power we see in a thunderstorm is the same as that we see in the movement of the stars.

Directivity

We cannot conceive of the Infinite Intelligence and Power as permitting itself to be directed to do wrong, or to do anything not in harmony with its own purposes. It goes without saying, that if there is intelligent directivity manifested in the universe, then there must be a purpose and a will behind the universe; and we see that Omnipotence cannot be led by a finite mind to thwart its own purposes or to take a course contrary to its own will. Therefore, suppose we start with this assumption: Man may direct infinite power, so long as man's purposes have the sanction of infinite intelligence. And we may add to it this further postulate: that man may draw upon infinite intelligence, if man's purpose is in agreement with the Divine will. Let us first give a little consideration to this postulate.

Abraham Lincoln was a pretty good example of a man who could draw upon the Infinite for knowledge. When, at the time of his first inauguration, he entered upon the mightiest and most perplexing task ever undertaken by one man in the whole history of governments. Lincoln was regarded by his cultured and college bred associates with a mixture of amusement and contempt. Seward even made him what was virtually a proposition to take over the presidency, and relieve him of responsibilities for which his mental equipment was supposed to be inadequate; for who supposed that this man, who had "never learned" could have knowledge? But as time went on it was demonstrated that in every crisis, however complicated and perplexing the situation might be, Lincoln knew what to do. He did not need instruction; he required no teachers. He knew. His mind was in such close harmony and adjustment with the Infinite Mind; that what God knew, he knew. Lincoln had developed that greatest of all the attributes of the human mind, the power to perceive the truth. He was not "led." He was not "inspired." He was not a "medium." He was a Master; a leader. He and his Father were one.

The most valuable education, and perhaps the only education of real value, is that which develops a man's soul to the point of being able to perceive the truth. The great men and women of history have not been these whose minds have been most crammed with booklore. The mightiest works are done by those who know, without being taught by man. And, what is most difficult to believe: this knowledge may include not only abstract wisdom, but concrete information; historical, scientific or other facts; anything one needs to know.

I want to be definite and explicit on this point. Let us suppose that what you want is success in business. First, are you in such a frame of mind that your success will be worthwhile? Will it do you, or God, or anybody else any real good if you succeed? Do you earnestly want your success to help along toward the fruition of the Eternal Purpose? If not, do not waste time trying to find out things from God. Ask the devil; for while there is no infinite devil, there are plenty of finite ones, and you may find some shrewd one to help you attain that success which is really the worst of failures.

But if you are sure your will is to make your success worthwhile, you have a right to draw on the All-knowledge. Now, understand, you do not want any miracles worked. You do not want God to do your work for you; you are going to do it yourself. You do not want to be "led" or "inspired" to do things; you simply want to *know*. It does not at all matter *what* it is that you want to know. You may be a businessman, and want to know whether to make a certain investment; you may be a farmer, and want to know what to plant in the North field; you may be a physician, and want the correct diagnosis in a certain case; you may be a writer, and want to know whether a certain story about Napoleon is true, or if you had better use it as an illustration; you may want to know if a certain alleged fact in nature is really a fact; it does not matter what, so that the knowledge is really essential to you, and so that you and your work are worthwhile. *You* are always worthwhile, when your work is worthwhile. And your work, no matter how small, is worthwhile if it is in the line of the Eternal Purpose. He that willeth to do, shall know. The spirit shall guide you into all truth.

Well, the next thing is to consider methods - how to put yourself in position to find out what you want to know. First, don't be in a hurry. You are going to know this thing, whatever it is and you are going to know it in time. Hurry is the result of doubt and fear; and doubt and fear will shut your mind against the very information you are seeking. God knows this thing, and you are going to know it. There is no doubt about it at all; it is perfectly sure. There is no hurry; wait until you have put all other problems and distractions out of your mind, and until you are where you can sit for a while by yourself, without fear or interruption. Then sit down, and get ready. Assert your will to do the will of God. Declare your purpose to use this knowledge in a way that will be worthwhile. Now fix your mind on the matter; do not consider it, nor try to think it out; hold your mind upon the investment, or the field, or the patient, and wait; let your mental attitude correspond to that of a person who puts the receiver of the telephone to his ear, and waits for the other party to tell him what he wants to know. In due time a conviction will grow up in your mind; I will not make the investment; I will sow oats in the field, and seed it to clover; the patient has a cancer; the story is true. You need not expect to get the unnecessary and nonessential details; you will get the main facts, which are all you need to know.

The only risk you run is that you may mistake the convictions you reach by reasoning for those which are perceptions of truth. I do not wish to be understood as decrying or belittling reason; it is your best guide in all ordinary matters; but in the most important matters you have not sufficient data to reason from, and it is in these things that you must ask God. And when you ask God, be sure you do not reason out your own answer. It will take a little experience, perhaps, to enable you to distinguish clearly between the things you know, and those you think you know.

This, then, is the method of getting truth by intuition, which means inside teaching. And when you get it, the next thing is to act upon it - to go ahead, banking upon your information as positively as you do upon what you see with your eyes and hear with your ears. Here is where a great many people fail. They are afraid to launch out on the promises; they refuse to trust their first perception of truth, and so they do not get a second one. I wanted, once, for a lecture, a certain fact in connection with the early life of Lincoln; I got what I wanted in the silence, and asserted it positively and continuously; and several years afterward evidence was brought to light which corroborated my statements to the minutest details. I have had similar things happen many times, and I have discovered that I can find out anything, past or present that I need to know, or that I have a right to know. This is saying a great deal, but it is a fact that you can demonstrate for yourself. All that is past and present is in the Universal Intelligence; I do not know whether the future is there or not, but I suspect it is, at least to some extent. There is not much of the future that we need, or ought to know.

Methods

We now take up the question of the dirigibility of power. Can we apply the power of God to the solution of our own problems, and use it in overcoming our personal difficulties?

Yes, under certain conditions. The power which is manifested within your own bodies is not essentially different from the power displayed in the movements of the planets; it is all one. "It is God that worketh in you to will and to do;" your vital energy is one with the vital power of the universe. When you pick up a lead pencil or a crowbar you direct the universal power; and if you will create the right conditions you can direct it outside your body as well.

And what are the right conditions? Well, the first lies in the consideration of your own motive. You cannot direct the All-power to accomplish anything which is contrary to the dictates of the All-intelligence. You cannot divide God against himself; therefore, the first condition is a complete unity of your will with His will - the will to do the Will of God. Examine your motives and hopes, now, and see if they are such that you can call, with perfect assurance, for the help of God.

Now, what is it that you want to do? Let us suppose that you have a business enterprise to put through, and you will need to influence the minds and obtain the consent of a great many men; or that you are a physician, and wish to heal a large number of patients; or that you wish to increase the love of husband or wife, or to influence and save a wayward child. For all these you may legitimately desire to command the power of God. And now, as to methods.

First, you must know what you are going to try to do. You are not going to ask God, in a general way to do something for you, using his own methods; you are going to select your own method, and apply the All-power to the work, consciously and purposefully. Be sure you are going to do the right thing before you try to turn on the power. Get knowledge first, for knowledge will give you the second great essential, which is faith. You may get knowledge without faith, but you cannot use power without faith. It is the calm, unwavering, continuous assertion of faith that turns on the power; a doubt shuts it off. You see the steps are three: First, to submit your will to God;

second, to receive knowledge *from* God; and third, to assert your will *with* God. You surrender your will in order to get it back enlarged and made irresistible.

Well, you have gained your knowledge, and you are ready to begin. Hold in your mind the thought of the men whose consent you wish to gain, and remember that the atmosphere which surrounds you and them is charged with irresistible power, which is at your disposal. You are calm, serene, poised and perfectly confident. "This is the right thing to do; it is the best thing for all of us, and you will all do it, my friends; you cannot help it, for my will is concentrating the All-power upon you; when I see you, you will give your ready assent to the proposition." Do not waver from this assertion, nor depart from this attitude of mind. You do not need to think of your men individually, unless you feel that one or more of them are specially unfriendly and hard to convince; in that case, concentrate on them a part of the time. Do not be in a hurry to *see* them personally; do the work first, and when you do go to see them, your attitude of calm conviction will be irresistibly convincing.

In healing the sick, remember that the atmosphere is vibrating with Life and healing power, and that your will can concentrate it upon and about your patients. Hold them continuously in mind, and draw the power to them. Bear in mind here, the value of the impression made by your personality and bearing upon others, and cultivate an outward appearance of calm confidence and power. When you are called to a case of extreme pain, do not get excited, or over-sympathetic; do not get in a hurry to relieve it. Do not hesitate to use external means, such as hot or cold applications or counter-irritants, massage or laying on of hands, or to give harmless medicines or home remedies; any or all of these may help you in controlling your own mind as well as that of your patient; but whatever material means you use, do not for an instant falter in your mental application of the All-power to the work in hand. It is that which really heals; all the other means are merely accessories.

Coming now to our next supposition, that you desire to win the love of a husband or wife, we find the elements somewhat different, and a change in methods necessary. Love cannot be commanded; it must be won. God Himself cannot make people love you unless you are lovable. It is foolish to complain that people do not love you as well as they ought. Nobody "ought" to love you; nobody is under any obligation to love you, and if they were, it would not make the least difference. It is a mistake to suppose that people can be made to love each other by commandments or obligations. Suppose the government should pass a law that every girl named Smith should love a man named Jones; would the power of the state be able to produce the desired affection in the hearts of those concerned?

Before marriage we universally recognize the truth about love. The young man knows that his sweet heart is under no obligation to love him; and he sets to work to *win* her affections. He "courts" her; he puts on the best and nicest looking clothes he can get; he assumes the attitude of a gallant, courteous, tender gentleman. And the girl does the same thing - or the feminine equivalent of it; and so they win each other's love. That is the way they do it, and there is no other way to do it, either before or after marriage; the same methods which win love before marriage will keep and increase it afterward. There is a great deal of twaddle written about "affinities" and the evil of marriage for life; marriage for life is all right if one or both parties are not too lazy or too selfish to take a little trouble to keep what they have won; and the husband and wife who try as hard to "affinitize" after marriage as they did before will always succeed in doing so.

But when you have made yourself as lovely as possible, you can call to your aid the divine power, and divine peace; you can fill your home with it, and surround yourself with an atmosphere that will make you irresistibly attractive. Try it.

In the case of our fourth supposition, the general method of procedure is the same. Do not follow, watch, or spy upon the wayward one; and do not preach or scold, or lecture. Be yourself, what you would have him to be; and calmly, persistently and with faith concentrate the Power upon him until you have produced the mental condition you desire. "And what things so ever ye desire when ye pray, believe that ye have them, and ye shall receive them."

The Law of Attraction

By Wallace D. Wattles

In this power-packed book, discover the steadfast, mathematical cause of success available to all mankind, and begin to apply it to YOUR life today to produce the effects you seek. In these pages, W. D. Wattles will teach you how to KNOW, with certitude, that you can succeed, and will show you HOW to do so. The power lies within your own mind. Master the principles Wattles presents, and you cannot fail to move forward toward the attainment of your goals.

CONTENTS

PREFACE

The Universe is governed by Law - one great Law. Its manifestations are multiform, but viewed from the Ultimate there is but one Law. We are familiar with some of its manifestations, but are almost totally ignorant of certain others. Still we are learning a little more every day - the veil is being gradually lifted. We speak learnedly of the Law of Gravitation, but ignore that equally wonderful manifestation, THE LAW OF ATTRACTION. We are familiar with that wonderful manifestation of Law which draws and holds together the atoms of which matter is composed - we recognize the power of the law that attracts bodies to the earth, that holds the circling worlds in their places, but we close our eyes to the mighty law that draws to us the things we desire or fear, that makes or mars our lives.

When we come to see that Thought is a force - a manifestation of energy -having a magnet-like power of attraction, we will begin to understand the why and wherefore of many things that have heretofore seemed dark to us. There is no study that will so well repay the student for his time and trouble as the study of the workings of this mighty law of the world of Thought - the Law of Attraction. When we think we send out vibrations of a fine ethereal substance, which are as real as the vibrations manifesting light, heat, electricity, magnetism. That these vibrations are not evident to our five senses is no proof that they do not exist. A powerful magnet will send out vibrations and exert a force sufficient to attract to itself a piece of steel weighing a hundred pounds, but we can neither see, taste, smell, hear nor feel the mighty force. These thought vibrations, likewise, cannot be seen, tasted, smelled, heard nor felt in the ordinary way; although it is true there are on record cases of persons peculiarly sensitive to psychic impressions who have perceived powerful thought-waves, and very many of us can testify that we have distinctly felt the thought vibrations of others, both whilst in the presence of the sender and at a distance. Telepathy and its kindred phenomena are not idle dreams. Light and heat are manifested by vibrations of a far lower intensity than those of Thought, but the difference is solely in the rate of vibration. The annals of science throw an interesting light upon this question. Prof. Elisha Gray, an eminent scientist, says in his little book, "The Miracles of Nature": "There is much food for speculation in the thought that there exist sound-waves that no human ear can hear, and color-waves of light that no eye can see. The long, dark, soundless space between 40,000 and 400,000,000,000,000 vibrations per second, and the infinity of range beyond 700,000,000,000,000 vibrations per second, where light ceases, in the universe of motion, makes it possible to indulge in speculation."

M. M. Williams, in his work entitled "Short Chapters in Science," says: "There is no gradation between the most rapid undulations or tremblings that produce our sensation of sound, and the slowest of those which give rise to our sensations of gentlest warmth. There is a huge gap between them, wide enough to include another world of motion, all lying between our world of sound and our world of heat and light; and there is no good reason whatever for supposing that matter is incapable of such intermediate activity, or that such activity may not give rise to intermediate sensations, provided there are organs for taking up and sensifying their movements." I cite the above authorities merely to give you food for thought, not to attempt to demonstrate to you the fact that thought vibrations exist. The last-named fact has been fully established to the satisfaction of numerous investigators of the subject, and a little reflection will show you that it coincides with your own experiences. We often hear repeated the well-known Mental Science statement, "Thoughts are Things," and we say these words over without consciously realizing just what is the meaning of the statement. If we fully comprehended the truth of the statement and the natural consequences of the truth back of it, we should understand many things which have appeared dark to us, and would be able to use the wonderful power, Thought Force, just as we use any other manifestation of Energy. As I have said, when we think we set into motion vibrations of a very high degree, but just as real as the vibrations of light, heat, sound, electricity. And when we understand the laws governing the production and transmission of these vibrations we will be able to use them in our daily life, just as we do the better known forms of energy. That we cannot see, hear, weigh or measure these vibrations is no proof that they do not exist. There exist waves of sound which no human ear can hear, although some of these are undoubtedly registered by the ear of some of the insects, and others are caught by delicate scientific instruments invented by man; yet there is a great gap between the sounds registered by the most delicate instrument and the limit which man's mind, reasoning by analogy, knows to be the boundary line between sound waves and some other forms of vibration. And there are light waves which the eye of man does not register, some of which may be detected by more delicate instruments, and many more so fine that the instrument has not yet been invented which will detect them, although improvements are being made every year and the unexplored field gradually lessened. As new instruments are invented, new vibrations are registered by them -and yet the vibrations were just as real before the invention of the instrument as afterward. Supposing that we had no instruments to register magnetism - one might be justified in denying the existence of that mighty force, because it could not be tasted, felt, smelt, heard, seen, weighted or measured. And yet the mighty magnet would still send out waves of force sufficient to draw to it pieces of steel weighing hundreds of pounds. Each form of vibration requires its own form of instrument for registration. At present the human brain seems to be the only instrument capable of registering thought waves, although occultists say that in this century scientists will invent apparatus sufficiently delicate to catch and register such impressions. And from present indications it looks as if the invention named might be expected at any time. The demand exists and undoubtedly will be soon supplied. But to those who have experimented along the lines of practical telepathy no further proof is required than the results of their own experiments. We are sending out thoughts of greater or less intensity all the time, and we are reaping the results of such thoughts. Not only do our thought waves influence ourselves and others, but they have a drawing power -they attract to us the thoughts of others, things, circumstances, people, "luck," in accord with the character of the thought uppermost in our minds. Thoughts of Love will attract to us the Love of others; circumstances and surroundings in accord with the thought; people who are of like thought. Thoughts of Anger, Hate, Envy, Malice and Jealousy will draw to us the foul brood of kindred thoughts emanating from the minds of others; circumstances in which we will be called upon to manifest these vile thoughts and will receive them in turn from others; people who will manifest inharmony; and so on. A strong thought or a thought long continued, will make us the center of attraction for the corresponding thought waves of others. Like attracts like in the Thought World - as ye sow so shall ye reap. Birds of a feather flock together in the Thought World - curses like chickens come home to roost, and bringing their friends with them. The man or woman who is filled with Love sees Love on all sides and attracts the Love of others. The man with hate in his heart gets all the Hate he can stand. The man who thinks Fight generally runs up against all the

Fight he wants before he gets through. And so it goes, each gets what he calls for over the wireless telegraphy of the Mind. The man who rises in the morning feeling "grumpy" usually manages to have the whole family in the same mood before the breakfast is over. The "nagging" woman generally finds enough to gratify her "nagging" propensity during the day. This matter of Thought Attraction is a serious one. When you stop to think of it you will see that a man really makes his own surroundings, although he blames others for it. I have known people who understood this law to hold a positive, calm thought and be absolutely unaffected by the inharmony surrounding them. They were like the vessel from which the oil had been poured on the troubled waters - they rested safely and calmly whilst the tempest raged around them. One is not at the mercy of the fitful storms of Thought after he has learned the workings of the Law. We have passed through the age of physical force on to the age of intellectual supremacy, and are now entering a new and almost unknown field, that of psychic power. This field has its established laws and we should acquaint ourselves with them or we will be crowded to the wall as are the ignorant on the planes of effort. I will endeavor to make plain to you the great underlying principles of this new field of energy which is opening up before us, that you may be able to make use of this great power and apply it for legitimate and worthy purposes, just as men are using steam, electricity and other forms of energy today.

William W. Atkinson

Chapter 1

Getting what you want is success; and success is an effect, coming from the application of a cause. Success is essentially the same in all cases; the difference is in the things the successful people want, but not in the success. Success is essentially the same, whether it results in the attainment of health, wealth, development or position; success is attainment, without regard to the things attained. And it is a law in nature that like causes always produce like effects; therefore, since success is the same in all cases, the cause of success must be the same in all cases.

The cause of success is always in the person who succeeds; you will see that this must be true, because if the cause of success were in nature, outside the person, then all persons similarly situated would succeed. The cause of success is not in the environment of the individual, because if it were, all persons within a given radius would be successful, and success would be wholly a matter of neighborhood; and we see that people whose environments are practically the same, and who live in the same neighborhood show us all degrees of success and failure; therefore, we know that the cause of success must be in the individual, and nowhere else.

It is, therefore, mathematically certain that you can succeed if you will find out the cause of success, and develop it to sufficient strength, and apply it properly to your work; for the application of a sufficient cause can not fail to produce a given effect. If there is a failure anywhere, of any kind, it is because the cause was either not sufficient or was not properly applied. The cause of success is some power within you; you have the power to develop any power to a limitless extent; for there is no end to mental growth; you can increase the strength of this power indefinitely, and so you can make it strong enough to do what you want to do, and to get what you want to get; when it is strong enough you can learn how to apply it to the work, and therefore, you can certainly succeed. All you have to learn is what is the cause of success, and how it must be applied.

The development of the special faculties to be used in your work is essential. We do not expect any one to succeed as a musician without developing the musical faculty; and it would be absurd to expect a machinist to succeed without developing the mechanical faculty, a clergyman to succeed without developing spiritual understanding and the use of words, or a banker to succeed without developing the faculty of finance. And in choosing a business, you should choose the one which will call for the use of your strongest faculties. If you have good mechanical ability, and are not spiritually minded and have no command of language, do not try to preach; and if you have the taste and talent to combine colors and fabrics into beautiful creation in millinery and dress, do not learn typewriting or stenography; get into a business which will use your strongest faculties, and develop these faculties all you can; and even this is not enough to insure success.

There are people with fine musical talent who fail as musicians; with good mechanical ability who fail as carpenters, blacksmiths and machinists; with deep spirituality and fluent use of language who fail as clergymen; with keen and logical minds who fail as lawyers, and so on; the special faculties used in your work are the tools you use, but success does not depend alone on having good tools; it depends more on the power which uses and applies the tools. Be sure that your tools are the best and kept in the best condition; you can cultivate any faculty to any desired extent.

The application of the musical faculty causes success in music; that of the mechanical faculty causes success in mechanical pursuits; that of the financial faculty causes success in banking, and so on; and the something which applies these faculties, or causes them to be applied is the cause of success. The faculties are tools; the user of the tools is you, yourself; that in you which can cause you to use the tools in the right way, at the right time and in the right place is the cause of success. What is this something in the person which causes him to use his faculties successfully?

What it is and how to develop it will be fully explained in the next section; but before taking that up you should read this section over several times, so as to fix upon your mind the impregnable logic of the statement that you can succeed. You can; and if you study the foregoing argument well, you will be convinced that you can; and to become convinced that you can succeed is the first requisite to success.

Chapter 2

The faculties of the human mind are the tools with which success is attained, and the right application of these tools to your work or business will do it successfully and get what you want. A few people succeed because they use their faculties successfully, and the majority, who have equally good faculties, fail because they use them unsuccessfully. There is something in the man who succeeds which enables him to use his faculties successfully, and this something must be cultivated by all who succeed. The question is: What is it?

It is hard to find a word which shall express it, and not be misleading. This something is Poise; and poise is peace and power combined; but it is more than poise, for poise is a condition, and this something is an action as well as a condition. This Something is Faith; but it is more than faith, as faith is commonly understood: As commonly understood, faith consists in the action of believing things which cannot be proved; and the Something which causes success is more than that.

It is Conscious Power in Action. It is ACTIVE POWER-CONSCIOUSNESS.

Power-Consciousness is what you feel when you know that you can do a thing; and you know HOW to do the thing. If I can cause you to KNOW that you can succeed, and to know that you know HOW to succeed, I have placed success within your grasp; for if you know that you can do a thing and know that you know how to do it, it is impossible that you should fail to do it, if you really try. When you are in full Power-Consciousness, you will approach the task in an absolutely successful frame of mind. Every thought will be a successful thought, every action a successful action; and if every thought and action is successful, the sum-total of all your actions cannot be failure.

What I have to do in these lessons, then, is to teach you how to create Power-Consciousness in yourself, so that you will know that you can do what you want to do and then to teach you how to do what you want to do. Read again the preceding section; it proves by unanswerable logic that you CAN succeed. It shows that all that is in any mind is in your mind; the difference, if any, being in development. It is a fact in nature that the undeveloped is always capable of development; we see then that the cause of success is in you, and is capable of full development. Having read this you must believe that it is possible for you to succeed; but it is not enough for you to believe that you can; you must know that you can; and the sub-conscious mind must know it as well as the objective mind.

People have a way of saying, "he can who thinks he can"; but this is not true. It is not even true that he can who knows he can, if only the objective mind is spoken of; for the sub-conscious mind will often completely set aside and overcome what is positively known by the objective mind. It is a true statement, however, that he can whose sub-conscious mind knows that he can; and it is especially true if his objective mind has been trained to do the work. People fail because they think, objectively, that they can do things, but do not know, subconsciously, that they can do them. It is more than likely that your subconscious mind is even now impressed with doubts of your ability to succeed; and these must be removed, or it will withhold its power when you need it most.

The sub-conscious mind is the source from which power comes in the action of any faculty; and a doubt will cause this power to be withheld, and the action will be weak; therefore, your first step must be to impress your sub-conscious mind with that fact that you CAN. This must be done by repeated suggestions. Practice the following mental exercise several times a day, and especially just before going to sleep; think quietly about the sub-conscious mentality, which permeates your whole body as water permeates a sponge; as you think of this mind, try to feel it; you will soon be able to become conscious of it. Hold this consciousness, and say with deep, earnest feeling: "I CAN succeed! All that is possible to any one is possible to me. I AM successful. I do succeed, for I am full of the Power of Success."

This is the simple truth. Realize that it is true, and repeat it over and over until your mentality is saturated through and through with the knowledge that YOU CAN DO WHAT YOU WANT TO DO. You can; other people have, and you can do more than any one has ever done, for no one has ever yet used all the power that is capable of being used. It is within your power to make a greater success in your business than any one has ever made before you.

Practice the above autosuggestion for a month with persistence, and you will begin to KNOW that you have within you that which CAN do what you want to do; and then you will be ready for the next section which will tell you how to proceed in doing what you want to do. But remember that it is absolutely essential that you should first impress upon the sub-conscious mind the knowledge that you CAN.

Chapter 3

Having filled your mentality, conscious and sub-conscious, with the faith that you CAN get what you want, the next question is one of the methods. You know that you can do it if you proceed in the right way; but which is the right way?

This much is certain; to get more, you must make constructive use of what you have. You cannot use what you have not; therefore, your problem is how to make the most constructive use of what you already have. Do not waste any time considering how you would use certain things if you had them; consider, simply, how to use what you have. It is also certain that you will progress more rapidly if you make the most perfect use of what you have. In fact, the degree of rapidity with which you attain what you want will depend upon the perfection with which you use what you have. Many people are at a standstill, or find things coming their way very slowly because they are making only partial use of present means, power and opportunities.

You may see this point more plainly by considering an analogy in nature. In the process of evolution, the squirrels developed their leaping power to its fullest extent; then a continuous effort to advance brought forth the flying squirrel, which has a membrane uniting the legs in such a way as to form a parachute and enable the animal to sail some distance beyond an ordinary leap. A little extension of the parachute jump of the flying squirrel produced the bat, which has membranous wings and can fly; and continuous flight produced the bird with feathered wings. The transition from one plane to another was accomplished simply by perfecting and extending functions. If the squirrels had not kept leaping further and further, there would have been no flying squirrel, and no power of flight. Making constructive use of the leaping power produced flight. If you are only jumping half as far as you can, you will never fly.

In nature, we see that life advances from one plane to another by perfecting function on the lower plane. Whenever an organism contains more life than it can express by functioning perfectly on its own plane, it begins to perform the functions of the next higher, or larger plane. The first squirrel which began to develop the parachute membrane must have been a very perfect leaper. This is the fundamental principle of evolution, and of all attainment.

In accordance with this principle, then, you can advance only by more than filling your present place. You must do, perfectly, all that you can do now; and it is the law that by doing perfectly all that you can do now you will become able to do later things which you cannot do now.

The doing to perfection of one thing invariably provides us with the equipment for doing the next larger thing, because it is a principle inherent in nature that life continuously advances. Every person who does one thing perfect is instantly presented with an opportunity to begin doing the next larger thing. This is the universal law of all life, and is unfailing. First, do perfectly all that you can do now; keep on doing it perfectly until the doing of it becomes so easy that you have surplus power left after doing it; then by this surplus power you will get a hold on the work of a higher plane, and begin to extend your correspondence with environment.

Get into a business which will use your strongest faculties, even if you must commence at the bottom; then develop those faculties to the utmost. Cultivate power-consciousness, so that you can apply your faculties successfully, and apply them in doing perfectly everything you can do now, where you are now. Do not wait for a change of environment; it may never come. Your only way of reaching a better environment is by making constructive use of your present environment. Only the most complete use of your present environment will place you in a more desirable one.

If you wish to extend your present business, remember that you can only do it by doing in the most perfect manner the business you already have. When you put life enough into your business to more than fill it, the surplus will get you more business. Do not reach out after more until you have life to spare after doing perfectly all that you have to do now. It is of no advantage to have more work or more business than you have life to do perfectly; if that is the case, increase your vital power first. And remember, it is the perfection with which you do what you have to do now that extends your field and brings you in touch with a larger environment.

Bear in mind that the motive force which gets you what you want is life; and that what you want, in the last analysis, is only an opportunity to live more; and that, therefore, you can get what you want only through the operation of that universal law by which all life advances continuously into fuller expression. That law is that whenever an organism has more life than can find expression by functioning perfectly on a given plane, its surplus life lifts it to the next higher plane. When you put enough of yourself into your present work to do it perfectly, your surplus power will extend your work into a larger field. It is also essential that you should have in mind what you want, so that your surplus power may be turned in the right direction.

Form a clear conception of what you seek to accomplish, but do not let what you seek to accomplish interfere with doing perfectly what you have to do now. Your concept of what you want is a guide to your energies, and an inspiration to cause you to apply them to the utmost to your present work. Live for the future now. Suppose that your desire is to have a department store, and you have only capital enough to start a peanut stand. Do not try to start a department store today, on a peanut stand capital; but start the peanut stand in the full faith and confidence that you will be able to develop it into a department store. Look upon the peanut stand merely as the beginning of the department store, and make it grow; you can.

Get more business by using constructively the business you have now; get more friends by using constructively the friends you already have; get a better position by using constructively the one you now have; get more domestic happiness by the constructive use of the love that already exists in your home.

Chapter 4

You can obtain what you want only by applying your faculties to your work and your environment; you become able to apply your faculties successfully by acquiring Power-Consciousness; and you go forward by a concentration on today's work, and by doing perfectly everything that can be done at the present time. You can get what you want in the future only by concentrating all your energies upon the constructive use of whatever you are in relation with today. An indifferent or half-hearted use of the elements in today's environment will be fatal to tomorrow's attainment.

Do not desire for today what is beyond your ability to get today; but be sure you get today the very best that can be had. Never take less than the very best that can be had at the present time; but do not waste energy by desiring what cannot be had at the present time. If you always have the best that can be had, you will continue to have better and better things, because it is a fundamental principle in the universe that life shall continually advance into more life, and into the use of more and better things; this is the principle which causes evolution. But if you are satisfied with less than the best that can be had, you will cease to move forward.

Ever transaction and relation of today whether it be business, domestic or social, must be made a stepping stone to what you want in the future; and to accomplish this you must put into each more than enough life to fill it. There must be surplus power in everything you do. It is this surplus power which causes advancement and gets you what you want; where there is no surplus power there is no advancement and no attainment. It is the surplus of life above and beyond the functions of present environment which causes evolution; and evolution is advancing into more life, or getting what you want.

Suppose, for instance, you are in trade or a profession, and wish to increase your business; it will not do, when you sell goods or service to make the matter a merely perfunctory transaction, taking the customer's money, giving him good value, and letting him go away feeling that you had no interest in the matter beyond giving him a fair deal and profiting thereby. Unless he feels that you have a personal interest in him and his needs, and that you are honestly desirous to increase his welfare, you have made a failure and are losing ground. When you can make every customer feel that you are really trying to advance his interests as well as your own, your business will grow. It is not necessary to give premiums, or heavier weights or better values than others give to accomplish this; it is done by putting life and interest into every transaction, however small.

If you desire to change your vocation, make your present business a stepping-stone to the one you want. As long as you are in your present business, fill it with life; the surplus will tend toward what you want. Take a live interest in every man, woman and child you meet in either a business or social way, and sincerely desire the best for them; they will soon begin to feel that your advancement is a matter of interest to them and they will unite their thoughts for your good. This will form a battery of power in your favor and will open ways of advancement for you.

If you are an employee and desire promotion, put life into everything you do; put in more than enough life and interest to fill each piece of work. But do not be servile; never be a flunkey; and above all things avoid the intellectual prostitution which is the vice of our times in many trades and most professions. I mean by this the being a mere hired apologist for and defender of immorality, graft, dishonesty, or vice in any form. The intellectual prostitute may rise in the service, but he is a lost soul. Respect yourself; be absolutely just to all; put LIFE into every act and thought and fix Power-Conscious thought upon the fact that you are entitled to promotion; it will come as soon as you can more than fill your present place in every day. If it does not come from you present employer it will come from another; it is the law that whosoever more than fills his present place must be advanced. But for this law there could be no evolution, and no progress; but mark well what follows.

It is not enough that you should merely put surplus life into your business relations. You will not advance far if you are a good businessman or employee, but a bad husband, an unjust father, or, an untrustworthy friend. Your failure in these respects will make you incapable of using your success for the advancement of life, and so you will not come under the operation of the constructive law. Many a man who fulfills the law in business is prevented from progressing because he is unkind to his wife, or deficient in some other relation of life. To come under the operation of the evolutionary force you must more than fill EVERY present relation.

A telegraph operator desired to get away from the key, and get onto a small farm; and he began to move in that direction by being "good" to his wife. He "courted" her, without any reference to his desire; and from being half indifferent she became interested and eager to help; soon they had a little piece of ground in the edge of the town, and she raised poultry and superintended a garden while he "pounded the key"; now they have a farm and he has obtained his desire. You can secure the co-operation, not only of your wife but of all the people around you by putting life and interest into all your relations with them.

Put into every relation, business, domestic or social, more than enough life to fill that relation; have faith, which is Power-Consciousness; know what you want in the future, but have today the very best that can be obtained today; never be satisfied at any time with less than the best that can be had at that time, but never waste energy in desiring what is not to be had now; use all things for the advancement of life for yourself and for all with whom you are related in any way. Follow out these principles of action and you cannot fail to get what you want; for the universe is so constructed that all things must work together for your good.

Chapter 5

Wealth-culture consists in making constructive use of the people and things in your environment.

First, get a clear mental picture of what you want. If your present business or profession is not the one most suitable to your talents and tastes, decide upon the one which is most suitable; and determine to get into that business or profession, and to achieve the very greatest success in it. Get a clear idea of what you want to do, and get a mental concept of the utmost success in that business or profession; and determine that you will attain to that. Give a great deal of time to forming this concept or mental picture; the more clear and definite it is, the easier will be your work. The man who is not quite sure what he wants to build will put up a wobbling and shaky structure.

Know what you want, and keep the picture of it in the background of your mind night and day; let it be like a picture on the wall of your room, always in your consciousness, night and day. And then begin to move toward it. Remember that if you have not the fully developed talent now, you can develop it as you go along; you can surely do what you want to do.

It is quite likely that at present you cannot do the thing you want to do because you are not in the right environment, and have not the necessary capital; but this does not hinder you from the beginning to move toward the right environment, and from beginning to acquire capital. Remember that you move forward only by doing what you can in your present environment. Suppose that you have only capital enough to operate a newsstand, and your great desire is to own a department store; do not get the idea that there is some magical method by which you can successfully operate a department store on a newsstand capital. There is, however, a mental science method by which you can so operate a newsstand as to certainly cause it to grow into a department store. Consider that your newsstand is one department of the store you are going to have; fix your mind on the department store, and begin to assimilate the rest of it. You will get it, if you make every act and thought constructive.

To make every act and thought constructive, every one must convey the idea of increase. Steadily hold in mind the thought of advancement for yourself; know that you are advancing toward what you want, and act and speak in this faith. Then every word and act will convey the idea of advancement and increase to others, and they will be drawn to you. Always remember that what all people are seeking for is increase.

First, study over the facts in regard to the great abundance until you know that there is wealth for you, and that you do not have to take this wealth from any one else. Avoid the competitive spirit. You can readily see that if there is limitless abundance there is enough for you, without robbing any one else. Then, knowing that it is the purpose of nature that you should have what you want, reflect upon the fact that you can get it only by acting. Consider that you can act only upon your present environment; and do not try to act now upon environment of the future. Then remember that in acting upon your present environment, you must make every act a success in itself; and that in doing this you must hold the purpose to get what you want. You can hold this purpose only as you get a clear mental picture of what you want; be sure that you have that. Also, remember that your actions will not have dynamic moving power unless you have an unwavering faith that you get what you want.

Form a clear mental picture of what you want; hold the purpose to get it; do everything perfectly, not in a servile spirit, but because you are a master mind; keep unwavering faith in your ultimate attainment of your goal, and you cannot fail to move forward.

The Law of Opulence

By Wallace D. Wattles

Learn the requirements for non-competitive success – the true secret to living happily in God's world. Since the purpose of nature is the continuous advancement of every man into more abundance, to be one with the laws or the mind of nature is to desire the advancement of all men at the expense of none. When what you seek for yourself you seek for all, then what you get for yourself – health, wealth, and happiness – you get for all.

CONTENTS

The Law of Opulence

The Kingdom of God

To live happily in God's world, the first essential is to abandon the idea of competition and of a limited supply. Too many people never entirely succeed in doing this. Competition in business originates in the idea of a limited supply. It grows out of the supposition that because there is not enough to go around, men must compete with each other for what there is. Many people still suppose that it is necessary that some should be poor in order that others may have enough, and believe that wealth is possible only to those who have superior ability, or the power to attract to themselves a larger portion from the limited supply. These people try to apply principles on the competitive plane, and they do so with a fair degree of success; they try to develop a superior attracting power; they inject new motives and new energy into competitive business methods; they assert, "I am success," all the while believing that they can succeed only because ninety-five per cent of all others fail.

The majority of these competitive people do achieve a great measure of success because their faith gives them just the energy, push and optimism which are necessary in competitive business. The confidence born of their belief makes a majority of their actions successful actions; they are exceptionally able competitors, and they attribute their success to thought-power and to affirmation when it is really almost purely competitive. This view sees only Caesar's kingdom; it has no conception of the kingdom of God. All the final results show that these people are only a part of Caesar's kingdom. Their fortunes fluctuate. They meet with losses and their business suffers from panics. Their prosperity is checkered by periods of adversity. Their sense of safety is mere self-confidence; deep in the subconscious they always carry the germ of secret fear.

No one can ever be wholly free from fear who recognizes any limitation in the supply, for if there is not enough to go around, we know that our turn to so without may come at any time. The lapses and failures of such people are traceable directly to the idea of a limited supply, to the idea that success and the attainment of wealth are possible only to a part of us.

Is there any truth in this idea that competition is necessary? Let us see. The things that are essential to life and advancement, mental and physical, may be roughly grouped under five heads, and these are: food, clothing, shelter, education and amusement. For three of these, food, clothing and shelter, we look to the world of nature for supply. These three with their appurtenances and extensions in the way of luxuries, decorations, art and beauty, constitute what we call wealth. Is there any limitation to the supply of these?

Take into consideration, first, the question of food-supply. In this country we have not yet begun to sound the possibilities of intensive agriculture, making four blades of grass grow where one grew before. It is a fact capable of mathematical demonstration that the single state of Texas, if all its resources were organized for the production of food, would produce enough to feed the whole present population of the globe, and feed them well. Our food products range from wheat in the Dakotas to rice in Carolina; from northern fruits in Michigan to oranges in California and Florida. This country, intensely cultivated, would feed the inhabitants of ten worlds like this. There is no lack in the food supply. When we pray to our Father, "Give us our daily bread," we should never forget to add a thanksgiving that He answered that prayer when He laid the foundation of the world. Remember, too, that the work of men like Burbank has but just begun; the food supply is capable of infinite development. There is, therefore, no need for men to compete with each other in order to get enough to eat.

As to the second essential, clothing, we find the same to be true. The United States can produce cotton for the world, but it is not necessary to dress the world in anything so cheap as cotton fabrics. We have sheep ranges to supply the woolen goods for all, and fields in which to raise the flax for fine linen; there are great wastes of land, now barren, where we might grow enough mulberry trees to feed the silk worms necessary to clothe the world in silks; we even have the deserts on which to raise ostriches for fine plumage. We have the resources sufficient to clothe every living man, woman and child in raiment finer than that of Solomon in all his glory. And there are undreamed of possibilities in the despised weeds by the wayside; some Burbank will presently develop them into the raw material for fabrics more beautiful than the world has ever seen. The supply of clothing is inexhaustible. No need to compete with one another here; no need for one to go in sackcloth that another may wear purple and fine linen; there are purple and fine linen for all.

Taking up the question of shelter we find the same conditions prevailing. There are great banks of clay waiting to be made into bricks and tile; there are vast ledges of building stone un-quarried as yet; we have learned that brick may be made of sand and lime, and that cement is excellent building material. It is an indisputable fact that a mansion finer than Vanderbilt's might be erected for every family in America, and when all were finished we should hardly have made a scratch on the surface of our supply of building material. No need for some to live in hovels in order that others may be delicately housed! And the supply for interior furnishings - for furniture, carpets, books, musical instruments, pictures, statuary, everything to delight the eye and mind of man is just as unlimited. Truly, there is no scarcity of things; nor is there any lack of work that ought to be done. There is no necessity in nature for competition, either for things or for jobs. There is enough useful and beautiful work waiting to be done to keep us all busy all our lives.

And it may be well to point out here that there is no lack in the supply of finished products because labor is not productive enough to keep pace with the demand. Modern machinery has solved the problem of production. The producing power of labor has been multiplied by six hundred in a little more than a generation. In making nails, for instance, one man does the work which required a thousand men one hundred years ago; and the same is approximately true in all lines of industry; and the end of the increase in producing power is not yet. There is nothing in which further improvement is not possible. Six hours' work a day, by all of us, would produce all that we all could use, including every known luxury.

With such abundance in the whole, we do not need to compete for a part; we do not need to take thought for tomorrow; we do not need to experience panics or reverses. We need only to seek for the kingdom of God, and His righteous relations toward each other, and all these things shall be added unto us. And what is the kingdom of God?

Leaven

The kingdom of God is in nature like the leaven in the meal - in all and through all. It includes all nature, for God is the cause of nature; and when nature is perfectly natural, there is the kingdom of God in all its fullness. If God be the Mind of nature, then there can be no more perfect expression of God than in the naturalness of nature. The kingdom of God includes all life, for God is the Life itself; and when life is lived in a perfectly natural way, there is the kingdom of God in all its fullness; for there can be no more perfect expression of God than the living of life in a natural way. And this brings us to the question, how may life be lived in the natural way?

The living of life consists in continually advancing into more life. Drop a seed in the center of a field; the life in the seed at once becomes active; it ceases to merely exist, and begins to live. Soon it produces a plant, and a seed head, in which there are thirty, sixty or a hundred seeds, each containing as much life as the first seed contained. These fall into the ground, and in their turn begin to live; and in time there are a million seeds in the field, each containing as much life as the first seed contained. The life of the first seed, by the mere act of living, has increased a million fold. The living of life consists in continuously increasing life; there is no other way to live.

This necessity of life for increase is the cause of what we know as evolution. There is no such thing as evolution in the mineral world. Minerals do not advance or progress. Lead does not evolve into tin, tin into iron, iron into silver, silver into gold, and so on. Evolution is found only in the organic forms of life, and is caused by the natural necessity of life to find fuller and fuller expression. Life on this earth began, no doubt, in a single cell; but a single cell could not give sufficient expression to life, and so it formed a double-celled organism; then organisms of many cells; then vertebrates; then mammals, and finally, man. All this because of the inherent necessity of life to advance forever into more complete expression.

And evolution did not cease with the formation of man; physical evolution ceased, and mental and spiritual evolution began. Man, from the beginning, has been developing more ability to live. Each generation is capable of living more than the preceding generation. The race is continually advancing into more life, and so we see that the living of life means to live more. The action of consciousness continually expands consciousness. The primal necessity of mind is to know more, and feel more, and enjoy more; and this necessity of mind is the cause of social evolution, and of all progress. If we take conscious life - as we must - to be the highest expression of God, or of the Mind of nature, then the purpose of all things must be to further the development of conscious life; and if man is the highest form of conscious life - and he is - then the purpose of all things must be to further the development of man. And if the development of man consists in the increase of his capacity for life, then the purpose of all things in nature must be to further the continuous advancement of man into more and more of life.

Life finds expression by the use of things. The measure of a man's life is not the things he possesses, but the number of things he is able to use rightly; and to have fullness of life is to have all the things we are capable of using rightly. The purpose of the Mind of nature being the continuous advancement of man into more life, it must also be the intention of that Mind that every man shall have the unrestricted use of all the things that he is capable of using and enjoying rightly. The purpose of God is that all should have life, and have it more abundantly. God is the Mind of nature, and God is in all, and through all; therefore the mind, or intelligence of God is in all and through all, like the leaven in the meal.

The desire for advancement is a fundamental fact in the action of mind, therefore the desire for advancement is in all and through all. All things desire the advancement of every man. If a man desires any good thing in order to live his life more fully, that thing desires him also. The mind of things responds to the mind of man, when man desires advancement. All things work together for good to those who desire only advancement. The greatest of all facts to us is the fact that there is a Mind in nature which desires us to have all the things we are capable of using, and willing to use, in the direction of fuller life, and that this Mind is in the things themselves, tending to bring them toward us; and that if we take the right course, recognizing this Mind and working with it, all things must come to us. But this

Mind is the Mind of the Whole, not of a part; and if we lose sight of the Whole and enter into competition with our fellows for a part we lose all.

For competition for a part is virtually a denial and rejection of the Whole. He who recognizes and accepts the whole cannot compete for a part. It is the idea of competition for a limited supply which prevents us from seeing and accepting the Abundance which is ours. We still keep up the foolish struggle of Caesar's kingdom, because we cannot see the kingdom of God, which is all around us and within us. But how are we to avoid competition, when the whole business world is proceeding on the method of competing for a limited supply? How can we get work without competing for jobs? Can we succeed in a competitive world without competing? Shall we withdraw from the world, and form communistic societies? Certainly not. To try that is to fail.

A communistic community is a body of people who do not compete with each other, but who do compete with everybody else. No community can be complete unto itself without greatly limiting its members in the means of life; and to do this is to defeat the end aimed at. And if it is not complete in itself, satisfying all its wants, it must compete with the outside world for what is lacking, and this is what we seek to avoid. No separation of a part from the Whole in any way, will solve the problem. The community scheme is inconvenient, unnatural and impracticable.

Shall we establish socialism and the cooperative commonwealth? We cannot do it, because socialism and the cooperative commonwealth are things of the whole, and can only be established by the whole. In reality, the co-operative commonwealth can never be established; it must establish itself, and it may take it a long time yet to do so. We cannot do away with competition by legislative enactment of any kind so long as the majority of men believe in the limited supply; so we must keep right on in business under the present system, and yet cease to compete. Can we do it? Yes. But how?

Abundance

God, the Mind of nature, produces the Abundance of nature with the purpose of providing for the development of man; not of some men, but of man. The purpose of nature is the continuous advancement of life; and as man is the embodiment of God and the highest form of life, the purpose of nature must be the continuous advancement of every man into more abundant life. That which seeks the advancement of every man cannot take anything from any man; therefore to be one with the Mind of nature is to seek the advancement of all at the expense of none; to seek to get for all what one desires to get for one's self. This must lift one entirely out of the competitive thought.

"What I want for myself, I want for all;" that is the declaration of independence aimed at the competitive system; "Our" Father, give "us," that is the prayer of the advancing life. This declaration and prayer are in unison with the Mind of nature; the man who so declares and so prays is mentally one with all that lives, God, nature and man; and this is the Atonement. To be mentally one with the Mind of things makes you able to register your thoughts on that mind, and your desires as well. When you desire a thing, and your mind and the Mind of things are one, that thing will desire you, and will move toward you. If you desire dollars, and your mind is one with the Mind that pervades dollars and all things else, dollars will he permeated with the desire to come to you and they will move toward you, impelled by the Eternal Power which makes for more abundant life. To obtain what you want, you only need to establish your own at-one-ment with the Mind of things, and they will be driven toward you.

But the primal purpose of the Mind of things is the continuous advancement of ALL into more abundant life; therefore, nothing will be taken away from any man or woman and given to you unless you give to that person more in the way of life than you take away. It will be plainly seen that the Divine Mind cannot be brought into action in the field of purely competitive business. God cannot be divided against Himself. He cannot be made to take from one and give to another. He will not decrease one man's opportunity to advance in life in order to increase another man's opportunity to advance in life. He is no respecter of persons, and has no favorites. He is equally in all, equally for all, and at the service of all alike.

To make the at-one-ment, you must see that your business gives to all who deal with you a full equivalent in life for the money value of what you take from them. I say in life; that does not necessarily mean in money value. Here is what many critics of the profit system fail to understand: that a thing of small value to one man may be of inestimable value to another who can use it for the advancement of his life. The value of a thing to a man is determined by the plane of life on which he stands: what is of no value on one plane, or in one stage of his development, is indispensable on another plane, or in another stage. The life-giving power of any article may be out of all proportion to its monetary value. This magazine is not worth a dollar a year in so far as the cash value of the paper and ink are concerned, but one sentence in it may be worth thousands of dollars to any reader. You may sell an article for more than it cost you, making a profit; but the purchaser may put it to such use that it will be worth hundreds of times its cost to him, and in that case profit is no robbery. See that your business meets this fundamental requirement; that is the first step.

When you have done this you are one with that Intelligence in nature which is working for more life for all. The aim of your work is that all may have life, and have it more abundantly. What you seek for yourself you are seeking for all, and the mental principle in everything that you need begins to gravitate toward you. If you need dollars, the Mind of things, IN the dollars is conscious of the need; and you can affirm with truth "Dollars want me." Dollars will begin to move toward you, and they will come, invariably, from those who need what you can give in exchange. The Divine Mind will attend to the transference of that which is needed for the advancement of life to the place where need exists. This will apply not only to all that you need to keep your business going, but to all that you are capable of using to enter into fuller life yourself. No good thing will be withheld from you. Your unity with the Evolutionary Power, with the Purpose of nature, will be such that you will receive all that nature has to give. Because you will do always the will of God, all things are yours, and you need to compete with no one.

But you must bear in mind that your wants are impressed on the Divine Mind only by your faith. A doubt cuts the connection. Anxiety and fear cut the connection. Exactly as you are in the matter of impressing your own subconscious mind, so you are in the matter of impressing the Mind of things. Your affirmations fall flat unless they are made with the dynamic power of absolute faith. The Mind of things will not act positively for doubt and hesitancy. "What things soever ye desire when ye pray, believe that ye receive them and ye shall have them." We cannot walk and work with God and distrust Him at the same time. If you feel distrust, you impress the Mind of things with distrust of you, and things will move away from you rather than toward you.

The requirements for non-competitive success are very simple. First, desire for everybody what you desire for yourself, and be sure to take nothing from anybody without giving a full equivalent in life; and the more you give the better for you. Then move out in the absolute faith that all you need for the fullest life you are capable of living will come to you. Pray with unfaltering faith to the Father that it shall come to you and thank him in every prayer, from a heart full of gratitude that it DOES come to you. Everything that comes to you will mean more life to someone else. Each gain you make will add to the wealth of someone else. What you get for yourself - life - you get for all. Your success adds to the life, health, wealth and happiness of all.

But someone says: Wherein does this differ from competition, after all? Are you not still competing with those in the same line of business? No! What you gain will not come from the limited supply for which others are struggling, but from the Whole. Let me illustrate: It may be said that there is only a limited supply of money in the country - not enough to supply the needs of all. Suppose a large number of people enter this Way of Life, and dollars begin to move toward them all, there will not be enough to go round. That is true, but the thought of need impressed upon the mind of things would react upon the minds of men; new currency laws would be passed; the bullion would begin to move toward the mints; and the printing presses to turn out bank notes if they were necessary to the advancement of life. The Mind of things reaches beyond the coined cash, into the gold and silver lying in the hearts of the hills; and it will all begin to move forward when it is called for by the prayer of faith.

And the same is true of everything else. Not only the mints, but the mills will start whenever a sufficient number of people have entered the way of the Advancing Life. If it be urged that the wage system prevents the workers from living full lives, the answer is that whenever the workers begin to live full lives, if the wage system stands in the way of their advancement it will be changed. Their demand for more life will be all that is required to change it.

Life cannot be advanced by changing systems but systems may be changed by the advance of life. There is plenty of work to be done in the erection of useful and beautiful things; all that is needed is a demand for those things by those whose sole purpose is to use them to give more life to all. As the number of such people increases, the prosperity of all will increase, and a constantly increasing proportion of all classes will come into the Truth, abandoning competition and the way of the limited supply, until the kingdom will be established on earth as it is in Heaven.

We have Book Recommendations for you

**Automatic Wealth: The Secrets of the Millionaire Mind--
Including: Acres of Diamonds, As a Man Thinketh, I Dare
you!, The Science of Getting Rich, The Way to Wealth, and
Think and Grow Rich [UNABRIDGED]
by Napoleon Hill, et al (CD-ROM)**

Think and Grow Rich by Napoleon Hill (Audio CD)

As a Man Thinketh by James Allen (Audio CD)

**Your Invisible Power: How to Attain Your Desires by Letting
Your Subconscious Mind Work for You [MP3 AUDIO]
[UNABRIDGED] by Genevieve Behrend, Jason McCoy (Narrator)
(Audio CD)**

**Thought Vibration or the Law of Attraction in the Thought
World & Your Invisible Power (Paperback)**

**The Law of Success, Volume I: The Principles of Self-Mastery by
Napoleon Hill (Paperback)**

**BN Publishing
Improving People's Life**

www.bnpublishing.com

Printed in the United Kingdom
by Lightning Source UK Ltd.
122844UK00001B/45-48/A